STORM WITHOUT A BREEZE

And other plays from
St. Kitts W.I.

Clement "Bouncin'" Williams

AuthorHouse™ LLC
1663 Liberty Drive
Bloomington, IN 47403
www.authorhouse.com
Phone: 1-800-839-8640

Published by AuthorHouse 06/23/2014

ISBN: 978-1-4969-1539-9 (sc)
ISBN: 978-1-4969-1538-2 (hc)
ISBN: 978-1-4969-1537-5 (e)

Library of Congress Control Number: 2014909894

STORM WITHOUT A BREEZE is a full length sociological commentary on the life and times of the late 1970's. even though some thirty years have transpired between the initial production and 2014 when this play will be first published in print, the issues of the play are still very relevant in the historical, social and political life of St. Kitts and Nevis and to the wider Caribbean and the world at large.

The play depicts two 24hour periods in the life of the protagonist Alric Mac some ten weeks apart. It reflects some of the issues of concern of the day and simply holds up a mirror for us to see some of the evils that are perpetrated in our society daily.

CHARACTERS

Alric Mac:
A middle age gentleman well educated with brilliant academic record, senior Civil Servant who has reached the position of Permanent Secretary in his Ministry and who lives in a posh upper-middle class neighborhood.

Maria:
She is a sexy looking young woman, in her mid to late twenties, has limited education maybe to basic high school level and is the kept mistress of Alric Mac.

Rev Mac:
He is the older brother to Alric and who is also a minister of religion.

Suzette:
She is the seventeen year old daughter of Alric Mac; a high school student and netballer.

Madge:
She appears as the ghost of Alric Mac's wife, who had been dead for several years.

Gwen:
She is the domestic servant of Alric and works fulltime at his home. She is early to mid thirties and has an above average body size,

Esrick:
He is in his early to mid thirties, works as a government messenger in Alric Mac's office and eventually builds a relationship with Gwen, He is also a singer and guitar player.

James Wells:
He is a taxi driver in his mid thirties who has
improved on his basic education by continuous
reading and extra mural studies.

Political Minister:
He is a mature gentleman.

The first production of **STORM WITHOUT A BREEZE** was done by the **NATIONAL PLAYERS THEATRE MOVEMENT** of St. Kitts, West Indies in October 1979 and was staged at the Basseterre High School Auditorium, Victoria Road, Basseterre, St. Kitts, KN. This play has been staged for over thirty productions throughout the Islands of St. Kitts and Nevis over the period of some thirty three years 1979-2012.

The First cast featured (October 1979)

Alric Mac . . . . Ken Martin
Maria . . . . Ruth Connor
Rev Mac . . . . Franchette Powell
Suzette . . . . Rhonda Thomas
Madge . . . . Linet Matthew
Gwen . . . . Dawne Caines
Esrick . . . . Steve Skerritt
James Wells . . . . Errol Finch
Political Minister . . . . Romig Phipps

PRODUCTION TEAM

Producer/Director . . . .Clement Bouncin'
Wlliams
Stage Manager . . . . Romig Phipps
Lighting . . . . Linval Gumbs
House Manager . . . . Ashton Maynard
Sound Effects . . . . Bernard "BT" Rawlins

The October 2012 production at the Sir Cecil
Jacobs' Auditorium Eastern Caribbean Central
Bank, Bird Rock St. Kitts
Alric Mac . . . . Schneidman Warner
Maria . . . . Unoma Allen
Rev Mac . . . . Ramong Benjamin
Suzette . . . . Jamella Fraser
Madge . . . . Azuree Liburd
Gwen . . . . Fiona Swanston
Esrick . . . . Sylvester Wattley
James Wells . . . . Romain Belgrove
Political Minister . . . .Reginald O'Loughlin

PRODUCTION TEAM

Producer/Director . . . .Clement Bouncin'
Williams
Stage Manager . . . . Damian Maynard
Lighting . . . . ECCB Tech Crew
House Manager . . . . Jihan Williams
Sound Effects . . . . Bernard "BT" Rawlins

ACT I

SCENE I

The set is a typical living room of the house for an upper middle class civil servant.

It consists of a triple chair or couch in the centre stage. Two single sitting chairs down stage just left and right of the centre, a low coffee table down from the triple chair or couch dominate down centre. At right centre a dining table with four corresponding chairs. Downstage right a space saver with television, stereo system, telephone and other what-nots to make it look complete. A liquor bar upstage left and a lazy—boy recliner down-stage left complete the main features on the set.

Door up centre leading to bedrooms
Door left leading from front house
Door right leading to kitchen area.

The scene opens with Maria, a young woman about twenty-five seated on the couch re-arranging her clothing and hair. She fixes and examines her appearance several times in a hand mirror.

Maria

- I can't understand this thing at all. Every time I come by you, you always leave me feeling worse than before I come here. You always have some kind of excuse to make. When it isn't this meeting you got to attend it is some official you have to meet at the airport. Look . . . . if you think you getting to old to handle me let me know, because I am sure I could get plenty more fellows who even younger than me.

Alric Mac

- (*Appearing from the bedroom . . . . completing his dress—long sleeved white shirt and dark trousers*). Look, why you don't stop your stupid ness. It is not that I am running from anything but time is time.

Maria

- Time is always time for you. When you say you coming home by me to pick me up say for about six on any evening, it would be a miracle if these two eyes of mine see you before nine o'clock.

Alric Mac

- But Maria you have to realize that sometimes I might be busy or drop asleep after having a shower when I come home from work. You know that there is hardly anyone at home during those hours of the day.

Maria

- Check that, you are Mr. Always-Concerned-about-Time and yet you will still drop asleep. You fully well know that I am always willing and ready and waiting for you. If you had me anywhere in your esteem you would never stop thinking about me never mind to drop asleep on me as you always do.

Alric Mac

- Maria, you know that you are my love line. I always try my best to make you as happy as you can be.

Maria

- Once ago! That was before I develop properly. I use to make out with you but now you . . . you only leaving me half-the-way.

Alric Mac

- What nonsense you talking?

Maria

- (*In a very disgusted mood*)I am a young woman just twenty-five years old and right in the prime of my life. All you doing is just hum-bugging me Mr. Alric Mac. I think I have the solution to everything.

Alric Mac

- (*Approaching her*)What is it Maria?

Maria

- (*Emphatically*)I am going to finish with you!

Alric Mac

- You don't really mean that, Maria?

Maria

- What is the use of staying with you and I can't get no satisfaction out of my life with you!

Alric Mac

- (*Surprised and puzzled*)Maria you can't say that!

Maria

- Ah say it already and ah gone say it again. I can't . . . . get . . . . no . . . . satisfaction. *(Said to the rhythm of the popular Otis Redding tune).*

Alric Mac

- I have done my best to make you happy; I have rented a flat for you.

Maria:

- Yes, and you afraid to come in there whether it is day or night.

Alric Mac:

- *(With a sense of concern)*But you know the people in that area are very malicious. They take full notice of everybody's business and before long you will hear it on the road, gossiped by everyone that Alric Mac is living with Maria Jackson.

Maria

- I know it is that! You don't want your big shot friends to know that you "there with" a hand-to-mouth woman, who come out of a family with no high back ground, and one who did not go to high school or college like you or your dead wife. You don't want your friends to know that you stepping down.

Alric Mac

- *(In a very apologetic tone)*No Maria, it is not like that!

Maria

- *(Tauntingly)*The fact that I come from a poor working class family stifling your performance in bed. You are so concerned about everything else, except making me really happy.

Alric Mac

- But Maria, we usually spend some enjoyable time in each other's company at least two to three times weekly. You have an apartment with all the conveniences you need, flat screen television, video, stereo system, telephone, a big double bed . . . . name it . . . you have.

Maria:

- Well, why you buy a double bed and you don't come there to share it. A double bed could be a most heart-breaking thing for a single woman to sleep on. Imagine you have space to roll, and when you roll you don't have a strong body to stop you from rolling off on to the floor . . . . (*after a thoughtful pause*) I think I am getting some ideas what to do.

Alric Mac

- Maria, I am hoping that you are not entertaining worthless thoughts?

Maria

- Yes! Like taking another man to share your bed with me.

Alric Mac

- Please don't be so . . . .

Maria

- You see eh? . . . It's people like you who does make good woman turn bad.

Alric Mac

- Look Maria. (*in a low pitch voice . . . . almost like a cry*) I want to make you happy in every sense of the word.

Maria

- I know that you have tried but you still aren't trying hard enough.

Alric Mac

- (*Hugging Maria*) what more can I do?

Maria

- You give me every thing I could want to make me comfortable, money enough to buy all the clothes I want and pay the bills, but there are some things which a woman must have before she is fully comfortable and happy. You can't go in a store and buy it, with or without money. (*Walking away with style and flair*) It is the essence which comes to a woman's body when she is fully loved by a man.

Alric Mac

- (*Walking away in opposite direction*) You disappointing me with these crazy talks.

Maria

- Well is years now you disappointing me, so what wrong if I disappoint you for once!

Alric Mac

- (*Recovering from the shock*). Look Maria, it is a bit late. Suzette should be back at home any time now. Please, you will have to leave now.

Maria

- (*Sarcastically*)I know that you don't want your daughter little Miss Suzette Mac to meet the old lay-go Maria Jackson in your home.

Alric Mac

- It is not that Maria! You would have to understand the situation as it is with me and Suzette.

Maria

- I know that my presence here will corrupt your daughter.

Alric Mac

- Maria you know the story just as well as I do. Suzette is at the age where she is very vulnerable . . . . I don't want her to know that I usually have a woman here in the very house in which her mother lived and died. You must understand. At least to her, I must keep the sanctity of the home.

Maria

- I now see; that is why you seldom take me any further than the living room. It is almost always on that chair, the carpet or on the back seat of your car.

Alric Mac

- Please Maria let us not make a mountain out of nothing. It is getting late; I will call a taxi to take you home.

Maria

- Is so? I have reached the stage where I am not good enough to leave you house driving in your car?

Alric Mac

- Maria it is not that! Suzette will be home anytime now and I have something very important to talk with her and I must do it this evening. I'll come around by you, maybe say after nine.

Maria

- Maybe say after nine . . . . What is that? You don't have to meet this Minister man that coming in for the talks again?

Alric Mac

- Oh my! That is true; by the time I get him booked in at the hotel and get things straightened out it might take me until . . . (*Looking at his watch*) eleven thirty.

Maria

- And if the flight is an hour late as usual it is going to take until tomorrow.

Alric Mac

- No, I will come back tonight.

Maria

- (*Laughing*)Ha-ha. Half-past twelve will still be tonight. Fool me because I don't have no big set of education. I guess while there is still darkness it is still night.

Alric Mac

- Don't be so harsh. I'll call the taxi *(goes to the telephone, takes up a directory to look for a number).*

Maria

- The number of the taxi stand is 466 8294 and ask for the fellow James Wells who does drive a red and black Ford Torino.

Alric Mac

- *(Lifts the receiver and dials)* Oh hello! Circus Taxi Stand? Is this chap James Wells who drive that black and red Ford Torino around? (Pause) Oh! I did not recognize your voice man. I have a small job for you to do, come up to my house . . . . yes, Alric Mac at Wade's Gardens, you know where the house is? No problem then, see you in a few minutes, right okay. *(To Maria)* Why you so specially want this fellow Wells to come for you?

Maria

- He is me Cousin, we grow up together. Why I should give somebody else a job when I could give my cousin.

Alric Mac

- That is all you know about that man?

Maria

- Every Saturday when I go to town to buy from the market and grocery he does drop me home. Do you thinking that there is something funny between me and him?

Alric Mac

- I haven't said anything about that, you know, but if the cap is fitting you, you could draw the string. (*Pause*) Anyway it is something more important than that. I notice the other evening when rain was falling up to a little past eight o'clock, that same car brought home Suzette and the other night when I went up by the school to collect her up from their end of term party; he drove off past me just as I was leaving the school gate. I noticed something looked a bit funny by the way Suzette was rubbing her forehead. I caught her waving at him.

Maria

- (*By now, having packed all her goods back into her bag*)I can't say a word about what you talking Mr. Mac. I have never seen them anywhere together.

Alric Mac

- You haven't, but many have. (*Knock is heard on the front door*). Hello, come in.

James

- (A sharply dressed taxi-driver enters) Hello Sir. I am the taxi driver, James Wells.

Alric Mac

- I am Alric Mac and this is my good friend Maria Jackson, I guess you know each other.

James

- Yes, she is me neighbour.

Alric Mac

- Oh so? Anyhow drop her home for me. What's the cost?

-

James

- Well its twenty dollars for a hire up to where she live Sir, but I'll take fifteen.

Alric Mac

- Never mind that you take you twenty dollars. (*hands over the money*) It's okay with me. (*James exits*).

Maria

- I don't think you will have the time to see me again tonight?

Alric Mac

- (*Walking behind Maria to the door*) Oh my love, its real rough you know. I am sure I would not get the chance to be back home before midnight. Anyhow, I will pick you up tomorrow afternoon, after four.

Maria

- As I expected, so until then. (EXIT)

BLACKOUT

ACT I

SCENE II

The scene opens with Alric Mac sweeping the floor, then picks up a small plastic cover, a condom casing, looks at it then puts it in his pocket, utters a sigh of relief that he found it before any one else came into the room.

Alric Mac

- (pause) This life is so difficult; as soon as you feel that everything is okay, problems appear before your eyes just like a ghost. (*He sits on the couch*) My life as a married man was most wonderful, a beautiful wife and such a cheerful little daughter to make you feel like life is really worth living. But that old man Harold had her plumb-in-front, before she could recognize it. Just like that she fell sick and in a few months time, dead. Cancer like a great beast devouring its prey. Suzette was only eleven then. I had neither sister nor other woman family nearby who could at least provide Suzette with the guidance necessary for girls at that stage of their life. Imagine me giving instructions on how to control certain biological functions, which I as a man can never experience. Sometimes we had a number of maids; it was always some kind of falling out. It was either that they could not get on with Suzette or they were not cooperative enough to my liking.

Rev Mac

- (*Entering after knocking on the door. Rev Mac dressed in a dark suit with ministerial collar*) Hi Alric!

Alric Mac

- Eh!! My good brother! It's quite some time now since you have been in this area

Rev Mac

- Been kept quite busy these days, the church work. You know since we have one minister short for the district I have quit a bit of extras to do.

Alric Mac

- Well, sit down; you must be quite tired with that extra work you have to do.

Rev Mac

- Well I am not as young as I used to be. The local preachers are reduced in numbers, the old ones die and no new ones coming in. Worst of all you can't get any of these youngsters who leave school and college with their CXC certificates and Associate Degrees to take on the ministry as a profession.

Alric Mac

- (*Invites Rev Mac to a seat*)What you taking, Scotch or Brandy?

Rev Mac

- I'll take some wine.

Alric Mac

- Mateus or Gallo?

Rev Mac

- Mateus is just fine.

Alric Mac

- (*Sitting and sharing the drink with Rev Mac*) Well, cheers. Ah! What cause the big step down wine and not Scotch?

Rev Mac

- I just felt like a wine, maybe it is that I had too many of the harder stuff for the day

Alric Mac

- What are you doing in the city?

Rev Mac

- I came in to do some shopping and hand in a report to the Archdeacon. How is Suzette?

Alric Mac

- It is difficult for me to give you an answer. She should be home anytime now. I guess she would give you the best answer. It is the same all over with these youngsters; all of them want to be self-determined.

Rev Mac

- I am hoping that you have not given her a free hand to do what she likes? Well I must say that it is difficult to stop them from doing what they want to do but at least you could have given her an insight to the rules and punishments of the game.

Alric Mac

- I have been always very careful to caution her of the evils of this world

Rev Mac

- And, she has not been taking you seriously?

Alric Mac

- At one stage my advice was working one hundred percent, but lately things have changed.

Rev Mac

- Well, Alric, the girl is now sixteen and because of their own psychological development teenagers are not going to take everything for granted, and let's face the facts, the youngsters today are much braver than we were at that stage of our lives.

Alric Mac

- These days she looks straight at me and answers as she pleases. Her comments are of the type which you cannot apprehend her for, yet, you can see the elements of rudeness stamped all over them.

Rev Mac

- How is she getting on in school?

Alric Mac

- Her school work has fallen; instead of getting nine or eight CXC passes she may just make the minimum five or six. The promise she had shown even to the end of last term has been melting away like a naked block of ice standing in the mid-day sun.

Rev Mac

- What do you think? Is it her netball?

Alric Mac

- I don't think so; sports would never prevent anyone from doing their academic work. Look I played cricket, football and dominoes throughout my university days and I still managed to survive.

Rev Mac

- Come on, little brother; choose a better word than survive. You excelled!

Alric Mac

- Okay big brother you have said it.

   (*Suzette, a young girl about sixteen, dressed in netball gear with ball in hand enters from the front door entrance.*)

Suzette

- Good evening! Hi Uncle John! Daddy. (*She walks toward her bed room upstage centre.*)

Rev Mac

- Tell me? Is this the way you greet your dear uncle whom you have not seen for almost six months? Come on; give your uncle a little kiss, and let's have it.

Suzette

- Do I kiss you on the cheeks or on your lips?

Rev Mac

- Well what's the difference

Suzette

- I know that some people prefer kisses on their lips.(*Suzette kisses Rev Mac on his cheek*). Now for yours Daddy. (*She kisses Alric Mac on his lips. (Exit to bedroom)*).

Alric Mac

- That little girl is something else!

Rev Mac

- Well I think I might be leaving now.

Alric Mac

- When I am going to see you again? You must come up for dinner one of these evenings; just give me a short notice so that I can get Gwen to prepare something special for you.

Suzette

- (*Entering from bedroom*). Dad, excuse me for ten minutes; I am going down by Cynthia to collect a history book.

Alric Mac

- Don't you think that it is a kind of late for a young girl to be on the street?

Suzette

- Dad, remember that this is not the dark ages again, the streets are well lit.

Alric Mac

- Look at that short skirt you are wearing.

Suzette

- Don't worry daddy, I wont be raped by any one on the streets. (*Exit*).

Rev Mac

- You know Alric; there is something I want to talk to you about. A few days ago I was talking to the minister.

Alric Mac

- Which one? You big boss, the new Archdeacon? Hey man! Tell me something; why they could not appoint one of you local fellows? It is high time they stop this nonsense of bringing in all kind and all sort and class. I might as well add, race of people, to be bosses in this country.

Rev Mac

- It is not that minister I am talking about and please, I really don't want to discuss that one.

Alric Mac

- You are afraid of the truth and not only that you would be afraid of the responsibility if they had to make you Archdeacon. Ha, ha! Imagine that we are an independent country for over twenty five years now and the head of the predominant denomination in this country, not a son of the soil and worst still he does not even look like one of us. If I ever have a say in the order of the independent service he would never have the opportunity to say the opening prayers for this nation.

Rev Mac

- Alric that is not the point in view at the moment. I want to relay a message from your Minister.

Alric Mac

- (*Shocked*)My Minister, but my office is next door to his. We see each other several times daily. I am sure that I saw him after you spoke to him. What type of message could that be?

Rev Mac

- Alric he wants you to go into politics.

Alric Mac

- Me? Why me? You remember granny's words, ' . . . children stay out of Politics'. Those words have plenty of meanings for me.

Rev Mac

- The Minister wants you to contest a seat in the next general elections.

Alric Mac

- That must be nonsense.

Rev Mac

- He thinks he needs a good man to contest the seat in constituency number 12.

Alric Mac

- (Puzzled) Well that is one of the big boys' seats.

Rev Mac

- Yes Alric, up to now! But it can be yours by the next elections.

Alric Mac

- Clear me up; you got me in the middle of a jig-saw puzzle. What is happening to the big boy? Is he planning to retire or resign?

Rev Mac

- A well trained civil servant, the good old British diplomacy coming out. Look brother don't pretend. I am your big brother and your source of spiritual blessings on Earth.

Alric Mac

- Fine! Cut that and let us get down to brass tacks.

Rev Mac

- You know that there have been all sorts of internal rumblings in the governing party. And you know fully well that several of them inside the Cabinet do not exchange a word out side the Cabinet Chambers. The Minister is trying to put a team together to launch a new party. According to him he has had confirmation from four others inside the Cabinet. And is in search of others to complete his slate of candidates. He is targeting persons from within and outside the party regime.

Alric Mac

- Oh so! Ha! So he is forming his own party.

Rev Mac

- He and the others are working quite hard on a constitution for the party and a manifesto to campaign on for the next general elections.

Alric Mac

- What is going to be the name of this new party

Rev Mac

- The United National Congress for Liberation and Equality.

Alric Mac

- U—N—C—L—E—uncle! Tell me brother, how come the Minister could tell you all this and he isn't telling me a thing.

Rev Mac

- He is a bit uncertain of what your reaction would have been. He knows that that you have always been a stalwart of the Labour Party, and he also recognizes that you are not too happy about the present state of affairs.

Alric Mac

- Why he wants me to run in that constituency? The incumbent is very strong over there. As long as he is running, anybody else including me doesn't have a chance. They will have to count it a blessing if one is lucky enough get back their deposit in a three party race.

Rev Mac

- The caucus of the new party has done a fantastic amount of ground work. They are really looking for the best persons to fill the ranks.

Alric Mac

- Why me? I never expressed to anyone that I had any political ambitions. Tell me something brother, how come the Minister is not going to get the incumbent to join his team? It is common knowledge that the incumbent has had a major falling out with the PM, so it would be more natural that the Minister chooses him to be part of the breakout party.

Rev Mac

- Well, the incumbent has been talking very strongly about stepping down, and this issue of dual citizenship has added a new dimension to him continuing to be a parliamentarian.

Alric Mac

- The incumbent is not going to give up his citizenship. The challenges about dual citizenship have stood up in almost all the cases that have been brought to Court throughout the Caribbean. I am certain the PM will fight for new legislation to bring this issues of persons with dual citizenship to the end; by getting enacted some sort of a bar to prevent that. It should not be too difficult as it is openly prohibited in the Constitution.

Rev Mac

- You also have to remember that the incumbent is going to be getting about seventy five percent of his basic salary at the end of the month for his three terms in Parliament, plus he just celebrated his sixty second birthday—Social Security on its way. Not to mention that he has been quite active in reactivating his real estate, insurance and other financial services.

Alric Mac

- True, that will save some of the stresses that politicians have to go through; like taking the marijuana smoke in their faces when they go into the ghettoes to ground with the brothers.

Rev Mac

- Brother Alric, you are university graduate, you did quite well. Everybody was so proud of you when you returned home. Remember the headlines of the newspaper? "Alric Mac, son of the soil gains first class honours".

Alric Mac

- Yes, the honours were in Mathematics and Economics not Politics.

Rev Mac

- (*Rising from seat*)With that sort of an academic background your lot cannot be less than Minister of Finance in the new administration when it is formed.

Alric Mac

- It sounds more to me like the minister in fine ants.

Rev Mac

- Come on Alric, this is no time for jokes; you got to accept the offer.

Alric Mac

- My dear brother and Reverend in Christ. I know my limitations and I am sure I was not made for politics.

Rev Mac

- The old phrase from Shakespeare answers your problem, "some are born politicians, and some make themselves politicians and other have politics trusted upon them".

Alric Mac

- (*Rising with great emphasis*) Me? Politician? That word politics means lies, conceit, bribing and only promising. Politics also mean grudge.

Rev Mac

- It is not all that bad!

Alric Mac

- Let me tell you something; I work every day with politicians, I have traveled all over the world with politicians. They are very nice people, very helpful people, before that day comes when they take that executive oath, but after that day, just as if they were bitten by a vampire, a sudden transformation. They become vicious and evil, conniving and self-centered, sucking the life blood of the common man, a Dracula in full form.

Rev Mac

- Alric, you can show to the world that you are a different breed of man from those fellows.

Alric Mac

- No brother, man is man. You know how many poor old people come to my office door taking it for the minister's, with all kind of problems; problems for food, problems of no clothes to go to their grandmother's funeral, problem of no clothes and shoes for their five children, between ten and eighteen, who are in school. It is a good thing that they don't have to pay fees and buy text books these days. There was another man who came in, he looked as strong as if Samson was his brother, and he came to remind the Minister, that he, his wife and the rest of his family voted for him in the last general elections. During the campaign he had promised him a job as a prison officer, since his job as a security office was made redundant by the closure of the sugar industry. Wife and seven children to feed; to feed from an occasional, two and three days per week work as a casual labourer. The Minister knew fully well that there was not much he could offer, but he needed the votes.

Rev Mac

- Alric look man! You are a fairly young man still full of life and with your education and experience the contribution you could make to this country as a minister of government . . . .

Alric Mac

- (*A bit angered*) I could never be a politician. (Pause) . . . Before I returned home from university I had a choice of several scholarships to do graduate studies. I tried to delay some and actually had to reject some. I wanted to return home not only to be with my wife and young daughter but also to serve this our beloved country for a while. I was pushed first into teaching, I enjoyed it but that was not what I really wanted to do. I really wanted to do graduate work so that I may serve my country at a much higher level and with greater dignity. You know what happened then, The Minister of Education in the former government said that I had to return home to serve my bond before I would be given leave to do any further studies. By the time my bond was exhausted; I applied for and got the Commonwealth Scholarship for studies in England; the then Minister refused to sign the recommendation that was required. He kept the file on his desk for months without dealing with it. That was my chance, having completed my five years bond serving as a teacher of Economics at the High School. I really wanted to do further studies in Econometrics so that I may serve my country with greater dignity. That crashed my hope and dream to be called Dr. Alric Mac. If I become a politician it is the same wickedness I might have to pass on.

Rev Mac

- You don't have to be like the others.

Alric Mac

- Look how many youngsters who had their eyes and mind set for higher goals. But before long their eyes were covered with blinders so that they can only look in the direction the politicians want them to look. Soon, their minds become clouded with frustration, yet they toil on continuously for the love of this our mother land. I could never be a politician.

Rev Mac

- Alric, you seem to be very mad about this whole thing. I am sorry that I had to be involved. I guess your minister knew quite well what your reaction would have been; so he asked me to come around and talk to you. Anyhow, I could do nothing but report your very strong objection to him.

Alric Mac

- It's a capital N and a capital O, No to me and politic. Tell the Minister I want to go to heaven when I die. Good-bye brother.

ACT I

SCENE III

Mr. Alric Mac returns home from his official business, breaths a sigh of relief and then looks at his watch.

Alric Mac

- It is twelve-thirty! Ha! It is tomorrow already! Pleasant dreams Maria. *(Mr. Mac puts down his brief case on the side table, pours himself a drink of brandy and drinks it in a straight in one gulp. Sits on the couch in a relaxed position, the lights go down, dim, after a short pause the stage is washed in black light, then psychedelic lighting in slow rotation and strange lighting flashes in intermittent strobes reminiscent of the lighting of a discotheque and weird music, then a ghost-like figure appears)*

Madge:

- *(Slowly with a pause between each call)* Alric! . . . . Alric! . . . . Alric! . . . . Alric!

Alric Mac

- *(still in a daze as if asleep)* Uhmn! . . . . Uhmn! . . . . Oh hi!

Madge

- Alric!

Alric Mac

- Oh my God what is this? Is it you Madge? (*He rises slowly then moves toward her and attempts to hug her*).

Madge

- *(Raising hand as if to warn him off)* No! Alric you must not, I am no longer living in your world, I am now living in a world way beyond you. Please Alric you must not try and touch me.

Alric Mac

- But what is this? You are my wife.

Madge

- No not now. I left your world some six years ago. From the moment I stepped into the great beyond I was forced into marriage with the great Prince of Darkness.

Alric Mac

- What stupidness you talking? You are still my wife, How could be married to this Prince of Darkness?

Madge

- Alric you must understand that you are
  dreaming. Remember well that six years
  ago I took ill and died after an extremely
  short time. I collapsed and was in a coma
  for two days not knowing whether I was
  here or there, do you remember Alric?

Alric Mac

- Yes, I do remember.

Madge

- Sit down Alric. (*Alric walks backwards
  to his seat on the couch*). Yes, now tell
  me what has become of the two people who
  meant the most to me. Tell me first of
  yourself.

Alric Mac

- Well, physically I am quite well. In the
  six almost seven years since you passed
  away I have had several promotions, I am
  now Permanent Secretary in my Ministry.

Madge

- Oh my Alric! I am so proud of you.

Alric Mac

- I am sure if you did not die you would have been principal of the State College. Oh Madge, just let me touch you. (*He tries*).

Madge

- No Alric, no, you must not. Please tell me about your social life. I should say your sex life.

Alric Mac

- Well, I . . . . I . . . . I . . . .

Madge

- Alric, don't be afraid to tell me; remember I have been dead almost seven years now. I cannot do anything to help you. Tell me Alric.

Alric Mac

- I have no regular lime, (*she looks at him questioningly*). Well, I could say just one.

Madge

- Is she good to you?

Alric Mac

- I can say, yes.

Madge

- Tell me about Suzette. Has she grown well? Is she doing well at school?

Alric Mac

- Madge, Suzette is so much like you; there is a perfect match of both of your images. She is quite intelligent.

Madge

- Is she behaving herself?

Alric Mac

- It is difficult to say. Sometimes she is like an angel from heaven and at other times she gets very rude, back chats far too often.

Madge

- Is she looking at boyfriends yet?

Alric Mac

- I think I have enough evidence to believe so but nothing really conclusive.

Madge

- Watch her well, protect her from those wolves. (*wall clock chimes four strokes*) It's past my time, I must be back. Goodbye Alric. See you Alric.

Alric Mac

- Please stay some more with me.

Madge

- No, I have to go. (*Lights fade to darkness as Madge exits the stage, after a short pause the bright lights comes up*).

Alric Mac

- (*Still in his sleep*) Please come back, please come back, please come back.

Suzette

- (*Entering from her room dressed in pajamas*) Daddy, Daddy, What's the matter?

Clement "Bouncin'" Williams

Alric Mac

- Your mother! Look at her! . . . . (*pause*)
  Oh shit! I must have been dreaming.

BLACKOUT

ACT I

SCENE IV

Next day: Alric Mac living room. The maid Gwen is cleaning the furniture and hums a tune as she works. During the cleaning she picks up a strange object.

Gwen

- What on earth this doing here? If Mr. Mac does use these things he got to be more careful. Well, at least he careful enough because he using them.

  (*A knock is heard on the door. Gwen opens; a young man dressed in public service messenger's uniform appears in the doorway*).

Esrick

- Good morning.

Gwen

- Good morning, what you doing here?

Esrick

- I will give you a chance to guess.

Gwen

- Look, do not form any fool with me, I have no time for stupidness.

Esrick

- Ah mean, you can't expect me to talk business and I am standing outside the door steps.

(Gwen opens the door wider and allows him to pass in).

Gwen

- Now you inside, please explain your business.

Esrick

- First of all, Could I have a glass of cold water so as to cool my nerves?

Gwen

- What cause you to be on fire? Must be your sins. *(Exits to kitchen).*

Esrick

- *(Sits on chair, looks around, gets up and checks the telephone number)* Oh!

Gwen

- *(Returning with glass of water)* What happen to you? You see me for the first time yesterday and you start haunting me already.

Esrick

- The length of time I know you have nothing to do with it. It is that I like you very much and I am seeking every opportunity to get to know you better.

Gwen

- So that is the business you on?

Esrick

- You give me a wrong number, I phone about six times between yesterday afternoon when I saw you and this morning.

Gwen

- I did not give you any wrong number. If it is you who forget it, say so.

Esrick

- Anyway, ah-ahm, so is here you working?

Gwen

- Yes!

Esrick

- For how long?

Gwen

- Almost a year now.

Esrick

- Is so long you living in town and I never see you before? Where you live?

Gwen

- At Fry's Village. You never see me before because I am not a street woman.

Esrick

- Anyhow, how much they does pay you?

Gwen

- What you want to know that for?

Esrick

- Well is just a matter of interest, I was thinking how I could help you out.

Gwen

- Two hundred and twenty five dollars a week.

Esrick

- Only that?

Gwen

- As if you were expecting to hear more, you ever hear that these big shots do pay their domestic servants good?

Esrick

- You can't support yourself with that, having to pay rent . . . .

Gwen

- . . . . And support my old mother and two children back home in the country. Think about that. If I want to buy a new blouse it going to take me almost six weeks to save enough money and by that time, the style done gone out of fashion.

Esrick

- That is why you need a nice fellow like me to help you out.

Gwen

- Yes! One help me out already and is two children he left me with. You want to give me two more no?

Esrick

- Not so I mean! When is your birthday?

Gwen

- Next Saturday.

Esrick

- Ok. Then I going to buy a new blouse for you as a birthday gift.

Gwen

- You serious? *(smiles)* I hope you buy the right size.

Esrick

- So which house in Fry's Village you live in?

Gwen

- Look, I don't want you to come by me house to check me out.

Esrick

- Well why? You have a next man?

Gwen

- A next man? Well you ain't me man. Why you asking me all these questions for?

Esrick

- Ah mean, you have a man?

Gwen

- No!

Esrick

- Then we could be good.

Gwen

- Not until you keep your promise.

Esrick

- Look I am a man to my word and further more I could borrow me partner car and take you to the DISCO for your birthday.

Gwen

- Well then is a Disco blouse you have to buy.

Esrick

- Of course, sweetheart.

Gwen

- You aren't fooling me darling?

Esrick

- No, honey.

Gwen

- When I going to get the blouse?

Esrick

- Friday morning, I will bring the blouse here for you.

Gwen

- Yes, and I will leave some lunch for you too, but you will have to come early because me boss does come home from work every twelve o'clock for his lunch.

Esrick

- So that mean that we having a pre birthday luncheon special? By the way, you did not tell me which house you live in at Fry's Village so that I could know where to come call you.

Gwen

- Me ain't living in Fry's Village.

Esrick

- But you just tell me so.

Gwen

- Yes! But a move. Ah now living in Dorset; near the garage next to the water pipe in a blue house.

Esrick

- No problem then, I know exactly where that is.

Gwen

• Just let me know about when you coming that I could look out for you. By the way it is almost twelve, you better leave now.

Esrick

• But before I leave I have a secret to tell you.

Gwen

• About what (*Esrick whispers in Gwen's ears*). Yes, but as long as you ain't tell nobody, on me cheek!

Esrick

• Ok, but you gone have to close your eyes (*Esrick kisses her on her lips then sings in a calypso rhythm*)

Ah just meet a lady
She driving me crazy
Ah ask she for a kiss
She tell me take it quick
But don't tell anybody
Oh gawd a bound to marry she.

Gwen

• Is a good thing nobody around to hear him.

BLACKOUT

ACT I

SCENE V

It is the same day at Mr. Mac's living room.
Suzette is at a table with a book. Gwen enters
the front door carrying a packet of groceries.

Gwen

- Miss Suzette you not going back to school? It done past one o'clock a long time ago.

Suzette

- What Miss Suzette, just Suzette or Suzie if you like. Anyhow the answer to your question is no. I have some work to do so I am staying at home this afternoon to do it.

Gwen

- But your father might fuss.

Suzette

- The only way he would know is if you tell him. By the way, Gwen, you have a boyfriend?

Gwen

- Why you ask me that?

Suzette

- Just answer yes or no!

Gwen

- Yes and No.

Suzette

- Two answers for one question? What about the fellow who was here with you this morning?

Gwen

- Which fellow? Here with me this morning? Where?

Suzette

- Here in this house with you. I came home from school in break and I was in my bedroom reading, so I listened to the full story. Anyway, you don't have to be afraid; I will not tell my father a word.

Gwen

- You promise?

Suzette

- A promise signed, sealed but not delivered. Anyhow, a promise for a promise *(They cross fingers)*.

Gwen

- Ah promise.

Suzette

- You know the fellow who drives a red and black taxi name James?

Gwen

- Yes, but he is not my boyfriend.

Suzette

- I did not say that.

Gwen

- Oh!

Suzette

- He is going to come here soon to help me with some History.

Gwen

- History? What a taxi-driver know about high school History.

Suzette

- Because a man drives a taxi does not mean that he is not intelligent.

Gwen

- I know some of them who behave as if they can't even read.

Suzette

- James is coming to help me and you promise to be ignorant of what ever takes place here and do not mention a word to my father or anybody else.

Gwen

- We sign the bargain already.

Suzette

- As long as he is here, stay in the kitchen except that there is an emergency.

Gwen

- But Miss Suzette what kind of emergency you mean?

Suzette

- Fire!

  (*Gwen exits to kitchen as Suzette settles in to do some work after a pause; a sound of the door knock is heard*)

James

- (*Enters from the front do. They hug and greets each other with a shallow kiss*) Hi! What's going on sweetheart? Been waiting long?

Suzette

- I have been waiting not too long. I was anxious for you to come.

James

- This is a house and a half your old man got here, I dream day and night about living in a house like this; posh furniture, liquor bar, wide screen television etc, etc, the only thing missing is a piano.

Suzette

- We have one.

James

- Where is it? In the bath room or the kitchen?

Suzette

- Don't be funny. It is out for repairs and tuning. Anyway, would you like a drink?

James

- Some wine, please.

Suzette

- Chilled or straight from the shelf?

James

- I'll take it straight from the shelf? It will give me more heat to the body.

  (Suzette moves to the liquor cabinet) Suppose you father come here and meet me?

Suzette

- If you are the big man you believe you are, all you have to do is introduce yourself.

James

- How should I do it. *(Standing with shoulders squared and upright and a 'million dollar' smile)* I am Mr. James Wells, proprietor and driver of a public transport unit. My intentions are honourable and I am hoping that some day I will marry your daughter and help you to become a grandfather. *(to Suzette)* How I sound?

Suzette

- *(Handing James the wine)* If you drink this, it might just make you head level.

James

- *(Taking a gulp of the wine)* Ah! Good! What is the problem?

Suzette

- James, these days preparing for CXC examination is so hard with the amount of SBA projects and essays we have to research and write, they really killing us with a lot of work. For example the Caribbean History project that Mr. Edwards gave me to do I am having a lot of problems with it. The type of questions he setting you can't find the information you need in none of the text book. Mr. Edwards say we must treat it as a research project.

James

- If you can't find the answer in the books you have, how you expect me to know the answer to it.

Suzette

- Hear the question first before you decide if you could answer it or not.

  (*Reading from an exercise book*) (a) Give an outline of the military activities on your island during the first half of the eighteenth century. (b) Describe any outstanding structures evident of such a military presence on your island. and (c) how these structures contribute to the modern society of today.

James

- Well that's not too difficult. Let's see, the eighteenth century that is the period from 1700 to 1799. That is the period during which the French and English had all these wars for dominance on these islands. Those which involved General Hood and De Grass and the sieges at Brimstone Hill. The French over-ran the English first and some time later the English retaliated. Anyhow,

I have a book with the full story of the wars I will lend it to you.

Suzette

- How Mr. Edwards say that they ain't got no book with everything in it.

James

- It have book and it have booklet. I got a lot of material from a training seminar we had from the Tourism Department.

Suzette

- Well what about the second part?

James

- You never been to Brimstone Hill Fortress?

Suzette

- It was a long time ago and I forget the details and exactly how it looked.

James

- I could tell you about the Citadel, the Bastions the courtyard and so on but you would appreciate it better if you went and see it for yourself.

Suzette

- You want to take me?

James

- If you're not afraid to go that far with me.

Suzette

- Afraid for what? James what ever you could do to me up on the Fort is the same thing you will have to do to me some other time and maybe some other place.

  (*James and Suzette embrace as to kiss. Arriving car brake-up*)

Gwen

- (*Rushing through from the kitchen.*) Miss Suzette your father!!

Suzette

- James, walk through the kitchen and go through the back gate!

Gwen

- Quick! Let's go!

James

- What about the dog?

Gwen

- Dog don't eat dog.

Suzette

- (*Seated at the table with books looking studious*) Hi Dad!

Alric Mac

- (*After entering from the front door*) Where is he?

Suzette

- He must be in the yard; I think Gwen fed him already.

Alric Mac

- Hell Suzette, I am not asking about a dog. I am asking about the man you just had here a few seconds ago, in my house. I will find him.

(*Mr. Mac opens the kitchen with haste only to find Gwen with a mop and pail at the door*).

Gwen

- Sorry Sir, you can't come in here now, I have soap and water on the floor already. (*Shuts the door*)

(*The sound of a departing car is heard*)

Alric Mac

- The son of a bitch! (*Looks through the front door*) Imagine that you my daughter is having an affair with the scum of humanity a mere taxi-driver. That is all your ambition?

Suzette

- Dad you said it because you believe it.

Alric Mac

- Back chats, eh! Since you have been exercising like a big woman you feel that you are a big woman.

Suzette

- Come on daddy; say exactly what you want to say, not exercising but having sex like a big woman.

Alric Mac

- Shut up! . . . . *(slaps Suzette)*

BLACKOUT

ACT II

SCENE I

Ten weeks later. A typical executive office. This scene takes place in Mr. Mac's Office. A knock is heard on the door.

Alric Mac

- Yes! Come in. *(The minister enters).*

Minister

- I just wanted to find out if you had completed the matter that I sent to you this morning.

Alric Mac

- More or less, I think it should be okay but I have sent it to the legal department to check out the legality of the enterprise.

Minister

- Legal or not legal we must find a way to get it done, by one mean or the other.

Alric Mac

- As you wish Mr. Minister.

Minister

- By the way, how did your daughter do in the exams?

Alric Mac

- She got her eight subjects passes with distinction in Caribbean History and English.

Minister

- That is quite good. Is she going to the local college or you going to pack her off to one of the metropolitan universities?

Alric Mac

- She will go to the local college and complete the Associate degree in the areas of her choice and then later she could transfer. Maybe by then we could get our act together and have the local college upgraded to full university status.

Minister

- I guess so, at least we have appointed a number of the necessary committees in place and any time now we should start receiving reports on matters of accreditation, funding and other pertinent issues.

Alric Mac

- Other pertinent issues? Such as?

Minister

- The whole question about autonomy is something the Cabinet is seriously considering. We recognize that the University will have to co-exist with the University of the West Indies and that relationship must be well worked out.

Alric Mac

- We already have some regional models that could be studied like the University of Technology—Jamaica and that one that is being set up in Trinidad and Tobago.

Minister

- Well we will see how that works out. Hey Alric, you notice that the messenger boy Esrick is sporting a new motor cycle, one of these new fancy ones. He seems to be making a lot of money singing at that night club.

Alric Mac

- Yes Sir, I have seen him at La Palma singing and playing guitar. You should see the US dollars these tourists give as tips. He is doing quite well.

Clement *"Bouncin'" Williams*

Minister

- With the present rate of exchange he is making almost half of my salary.

Alric Mac

- No two guesses about that, he and I may be on par. What's even more, he pays neither Social Security nor the Services levy on that money.

Minister

- Man he is making too much money. You know what, call him in the office the office and let him know what General Orders say on the matter. Until. (*Pauses as he is about to leave*) I still want you to reconsider the reply you sent me by way of your brother.

Alric Mac

- What I have said, I have said.

Minister

- We will see later. (*Minister exits*)
(*Alric Mac sounds the buzzer one beat*)

Esrick

- Yes, Sir.

Alric Mac

- I sounded the buzzer only once, I do not want you yet, but I do have something to say to you after I have spoken to the secretary.

Esrick

- She is not here at the moment sir. She just this moment went down by the corner store to check out some shoes.

Alric Mac

- Several times daily! It is either she parading the town or you gallivanting on the sportish motorcycle you have on government time, for government pay. I think I will speak to you now. Sit down. It has been brought to my attention that you are doing another job,

Esrick

- No sir.

Alric Mac

- Do not tell me any lies boy. I have seen you myself, singing and playing guitar at La Palma.

Esrick

- Sir, I do not call that work or to say another job. I just go at the club for a few hours on the busy nights, I do not get a cent from the owners, all I get Sir, is the tips the guests give me.

Alric Mac

- Anyhow, that is a form of work. You make an effort and you get money in return for your effort. You know that persons working in the civil service for the Establishment cannot have a second form of employment. You are a civil servant twenty four hours per day and seven days per week.

Esrick

- Sir, but you will realize that with the high cost of living a person who is working as a messenger cannot make enough money to live off and worse still he would never be able to own anything what so ever.

Alric Mac

- Well, that's how General Orders go. I never drafted them. They were enforced since in 1921 and have never been changed.

Esrick

- But Sir, it is over five years I am working here and nobody ever let me see these General Orders. If they are the conditions which I am to work under, I should at least know them.

Alric Mac

- Now you riding motorbike you getting rude! What I have to say to you is you will have to stop the singing in the night club or I will take a case against you to the Public Service Commission.

Esrick

- Mr. Mac, in 1921 when they draft the General Orders even though it was a few shillings the people worked for, they could have seen their way in life. But today, even you who get thousands of dollars a month do fall short with cash. To be honest sir, for me to live a decent life I'll have to continue singing.

Alric Mac

- So you don't care about your job?

Esrick

- Yes Sir, I care very much about it. I am just beginning to get serious and care about life. Since I started going by the club, I talk to a lot of people from overseas and everybody tell me about the importance of a good education towards success in life. It is only now that I could afford to pay the fees for the evening classes at the Division of Continuing Education at the College. Sir, I would be glad if you can give me the chance so that I could try and get the education that my parents could not afford to pay for and to some extent, I wasted a lot of time in school.

Alric Mac

- I am sorry we have to play this game by the rules. If I give you a chance many more will follow your example. You are working in the Service, thousands are working for less than you, adjust your life style to suit your salary. Your problem is not the high cost of living but it is the cost of living high. I will tell you further the Minister is quite angry about this matter.

Esrick

- (*Angry*) But Sir, They have other people who have top executive positions in the Civil Service who have other forms of earning money. Shares in all kinds of companies, business, real estate, taxis, what about them?

Alric Mac

- That is not under my notice. The Ministry must be run by the letter of the Law.

Esrick

- I think any man is entitled to make as much money he can on the side, provided that he is doing his work, and not using government time. That is how Capitalism goes Sir! That is how Democracy goes! It would be better if I was living in a Socialist or a Communist Country. Then I would not have to try so hard because I would be getting all I need and all the education I want for free.

Alric Mac

- Remember that you are in my office and I am the boss here.

Esrick

- I don't want to be rude, Mr. Mac, but you are preaching one thing and practicing another. You working under General Orders too.

Alric Mac

- What do you mean by that?

Esrick

- Sir, rumours have it that you own half of the new bakery that open a few months ago.

Alric Mac

- (shouting) Shut up! That is not true where you hear that?

Esrick

- The truth does catch fire easily. It is an effort you making and is money you getting so you have another job too.

Alric Mac

- Esrick, you are rude and out of place. I'll report this to the Public Service Commission for in-subordination.

Esrick

- That is what you call Democracy and Equality? You have a right which I cannot have? All of us are born equal but the next great equalizer is death, and I hope for generations to come, they give you and your likes a grave at least six feet and six inches deep.

Alric Mac

- That's the most I will stand from you. You are suspended from this moment until the hearing, when you will be fired without a cent compensation.

Esrick

- The money you will cause me to lose Mr. Mac will not be enough to pay for the sins and wickedness you committed in your own house against your own flesh.

Alric Mac

- What sin and wickedness you are talking about?

Esrick

- You know quite well, much better than I could know. (*Pause*)Tell the Minister I say he got what he wanted, but man will survive.

BLACKOUT

ACT II

SCENE II

Next day in Mr. Mac's living room: Suzette is
seated with a towel wiping her tears. Mr. Mac
with brief-case is ready to leave for work.

Alric Mac

- You took the tablets as I told you?

Suzette

- Yes!

Alric Mac

- Are you feeling any better?

Suzette

- No.

Alric Mac

- It is going to take some time before it works, anytime between three and seven days. Just relax; it would work even better then. Remember to take one every twelve hours, so you have to take another one at nine o'clock this evening.

Suzette

- (*Stares at Mr. Mac*) Uhmn! Uhmn!

Alric Mac

- Why you look at me like that? It is not the
  end of the world, everything will be quite
  okay. We are all human, we all have our
  faults and will make mistakes. One thing
  though, if and when we make mistakes we
  must not live with them, we must correct
  them. I'll see you later. *(Shouting)* Gwen.

Gwen

- *(Appearing at the kitchen door)* Yes Sir?

Alric Mac

- I am not coming home for lunch, I have a
  luncheon meeting.

Gwen

- Okay Sir. *(Exits the kitchen)*.

Alric Mac

- Suzie take it easy*(exits)*

**Suzette sits up in chair and wipes her teary
eyes.**

Gwen

- *(Entering from the kitchen)* Suzette you not going to the College? I see all you friends dress down in they College uniform.

Suzette

- I am feeling sick and I am not going for the rest of this week either.

Gwen

- What is the matter with you? You went to the doctor?

Suzette

- What is wrong with me is none of you business, please leave me alone.

  (A shiverish feeling runs through Suzette's body and she blows her jaws as if to vomit. She gets up and rushes to her room).

  (Gwen sees the vial containing the tablets and opens it, reads the label, throws one in her hand, examines it and recognizes the tablet and replaces the tablet before Suzette returns)

Gwen

- Suzette I have been noticing you these days, you vomiting quite often.

Suzette

- That is so because I have a stomach infection

Gwen

- In-fec-tion! What kind of infection that could be?

Suzette

- What ever kind of infection it is, it is not your business.

    (Suzette storms out of the living room back to her bed room and locks her door).

Esrick

- *(Stepping in from the front door)* Girl I out here waiting since ten past eight for the high and mighty Alric Mac to leave. *(Suzette enters walks to the table and takes up the vial with the tablets)* . . . . Oh! Good morning Miss Suzette.

Suzette

- It is morning yes, but not a good one for me. *(Exits bedroom).*

Esrick

- *(In a whisper)* What happen to she, she ain't going back school or to the College in truth? So what you tell me look like is true?

Gwen

- I got more than enough evidence to believe is so. She was vomiting again this morning. You would not guess what she says happen to her. . . . She got stomach infection!

Esrick

- *(Jokingly)* Stomach in-fec-tion!

Gwen

- By the way, you not working today, where you uniform?

Esrick

- Girl, I am on indefinite suspension.

Gwen

- Suspension? For what?

Esrick

- Mr. Mac said I was rude to him. He says if I want to work as a messenger I cannot sing in the night-club.

Gwen

- Mr. Mac is not a man like that! How he could do that? How you will finish pay off for your motor-bike?

Esrick

- I will show all like Alric Mac, that they can't stop me.

Gwen

- But Esrick what really happen to you and Mr. Mac?

Esrick

- Yesterday morning he called me into his office and said that the Minister was not happy with the fact that I was making extra money singing. Then he started to talk about General Orders and twenty four hours a day Civil Servants.

Gwen

- General Orders, is the P.M. they calling General now?

Esrick

- No, not that kind of General, It is a set of regulations which people in the Civil Service suppose to be working under.

Gwen

- Why he say you rude?

Esrick

- I tell him that a lot of other big boy making outside money too, what really hurt him was when I tell him about the bakery he just open.

Gwen

- Boy, you mash he sore-foot. Tonight come home for me, we will talk things over, when I could curse him better. I don't want to curse him in his own house. Anybody could imagine that, just because you making some extra money. It is grudge they grudge you.

Well, I am going to spread what I know about his daughter around town. The shame that will bite him, he will be feeling worse than us. He puts you out of a job so he will have to feed you everyday. Call by the gate everyday between eleven and half past eleven for your lunch.

Esrick

- Gwen, you know I like beer, give me a cold one.

Gwen

- (*Exit to kitchen, then returns with a bottle and hands it to Esrick*) Make sure that you come back today for lunch.

BLACKOUT

ACT II

SCENE III

Mr. Mac's house. Gwen dials from the telephone. Another telephone below a sign marked—'Taxi Stand', rings in the far corner of the front of the theatre. James Wells answer.

James

- Circus Taxi Stand! James Wells speaking.

Gwen

- Yes, its me Gwen.

James

- Hi, what's happening? Suzette gave you a message for me?

Gwen

- No, she doesn't even know that I am calling you. Let me tell you something, she up here crying all the time. Something wrong with her.

James

- What that could be?

Gwen

- I am not a doctor, but from what I see you should have been the first one to know.

James

- I have not seen Suzette for over six weeks now, the most is a talk on the telephone and she did not say anything. What I find these days is that she always have some excuse when I try to see her, and even when she promise that I will pick her up she don't turn up. Maybe she just realize that I am not in her class or maybe she might be scared.

Gwen

- It is something else, you better come up here.

James

- I don't mind coming, but what about Mr. Mac?

Gwen

- He is not coming home now. He busy with some people from overseas. He did not even come home for lunch today.

James

- Well, it is two thirty now. I'll come now to make sure that I am out of there before four o'clock. I don't want to have

to tangle with that dog again. I have one
mark on me bottom already.

Gwen

- The other half wants a mark too, so that
they could match. Ha!

BLACKOUT

ACT II

SCENE IV

At Mr. Mac's house. Suzette is seated on the centre chair. She is crying with her head and hands buried in a towel. The door bell rings. Gwen crosses from the kitchen to the front door

James

- Hi! Where is Suzette?

Gwen

- Right there.

James

- Hi Suzie. What's the matter? What is wrong with you? At least you could look at me and say hello. (*James sit next to Suzette and continues to speak to her*) What on earth could be your problem? Come on Suzie talk to me, I might not be able to solve your problem but I can at least try. Look sweetheart, talk to me. Say something, anything. (*He touches Suzette, she gets up in a rage, takes a knife from the table and runs to her bedroom and slams the door lock*) (*James knocking on the door*) Suzette! Suzette! Open the door!

Gwen

- (*Entering from the kitchen*) What is it happening out here?

James

- Suzette would not talk to me. As I tried to touch her she got up took something from the table and rushed into her bed room. Look Gwen, be honest with me. What is wrong with Suzette?

Gwen

- You asking me? You are the best one to know.

James

- Know what?

Gwen

- She haven't told you?

James

- Tell me? About what?

Gwen

- You see how all you man is. Before things start to happen, the two of you used to be so nice. Now you playing you don't know what happen. You just like all other men ducking from their responsibilities.

James

- How could I be ducking from something that I am not aware of?

Gwen

- So you don't know that Suzette pregnant!

James

- (*Shocked*) Pregnant!

Gwen

- You don't have to get frightened so boy! Mr. Mac can't report you to the police, Suzette done sixteen already.

James

- No Gwen, It is impossible for Suzette to be pregnant, maybe she is suffering from some psychological disturbance.

Gwen

- These things are not always one hundred percent safe.

James

- Gwen it is impossible! I never had sexual contact with Suzette.

Gwen

- (*Shocked and amazed*) You serious?

James

- I swear to all the gods in heaven (*Kissing his hand and making the sign of the cross*). I like Suzette too much to encourage her into such actions. I don't have any need or the greed to make love to her. There are so many other women about these days. I don't want to confuse the young girl's mind; I can afford to wait until she leaves school.

Gwen

- So you were putting her up? Ha! Ha! Look, I have more than enough evidence to believe that Suzette is pregnant. All I could say is that somebody else picked the cherry for you.

  (*A scream and tumble is heard from inside Suzette's room. James rushes to the door which is still locked*).

James

- How could I get inside that room?

Gwen

- Go round the yard and jump through the window

James

- What about the dog?

Gwen

- Ah tie it already. (*James exits through the kitchen. He later re-enters from the bedroom holding Suzette. She has fainted and has blood running from her left wrist).*

James

- Gwen, get me some bandage or a clean piece of cloth. (*Gwen gets the bandage from a cabinet then hands it to James. He makes a crude tie so as to stop the blood from flowing).* It seems as if she tried to kill herself. Help me take her to the car; I will rush her to the hospital.

BLACKOUT

ACT II

SCENE V

Same day. Alric Mac's living room. Mr. Mac and Maria enter through the front door.

Maria

- *(As they enter)* Why you can't tell me what
  it is bothering you. You are complaining
  of everything. These days you are nervous.
  Your mind is not at ease! You have problems
  on the job?

Alric Mac

- No! I have a headache, I sense that
  something is wrong somewhere.

Maria

- It could be your conscience.

Alric Mac

- *(Holding his head as if in some form of
  agony)* Oh God! My brain is spinning in my
  head like a storm. It is a storm without
  a breeze blowing

Gwen

- *(Entering from the kitchen)* Mr. Mac!
  (recognizing Maria) Oh, good afternoon.

Alric Mac

- What are you doing here at this hour?

Gwen

- Mr. Mac all afternoon I was trying to call you; at your office, on your cell and I leave messages with everybody. Mr. Mac, James had to take Suzette to the hospital.

Alric Mac

- James? Suzette? Hospital? What for?

Gwen

- It looks to me as if Suzette was trying to kill herself. She cut her wrist with a knife. Luckily James was here so he took her to the hospital.

Alric Mac

- When this happened?

Gwen

- About three o'clock, I was waiting until you come home to tell you.

Alric Mac

- (*As if losing his nerves*) Nonsense, damn nonsense! That cannot be true! (*Holding his head again*) My head, oh God, it spinning . . . . It spinning like a storm

James

- (*Entering*) Good evening.

Alric Mac

- Who are you? You don't just walk into my house as you like.

James

- I have come to tell you that your daughter should recover from the ordeal she went through. We were lucky that the surgeon was still in the operating theatre. He patched her up; she needed two pints of blood which they got from the blood bank at the hospital. I stayed with her until she regained consciousness. When she came through she was answering the questions I asked her just before she made the attempt on her life. Mr. Mac, in the presence of several nurses and patients at the hospital, she revealed the whole story. The entire country will know about it before the break of the next dawn, this is what she said. (*James turns on a recording instrument and Suzette's voice, weak and sick is heard saying*) . . . ." **One night about six weeks ago, I was asleep in my bed, then suddenly I awoke and realize that a figure was crouched next to me, a pair of strong hand held me held me, I was about to scream, then a voice said don't cry it's me. I was shocked and I wondered why he would want to be in my bed. He started**

*to massage my arm, my back, my . . . .
Uhmnnn, I tried to get away from him, he
then said, come on Suzie be nice to me.
I could not get away from his grasp, we
struggled for a while, he overpowered
me then his body covered mine. He kept
forcing his hand between me, pulling at my
clothing. I could not move, I could hardly
breathe. Oh James I felt awful. Pains and
then and then and then uhmnn! Pains that
I have never felt before.*

Alric Mac

- Leave my house. Leave my house! All of you!
  (*Mr. Mac opens his briefcase and takes out
  a pistol. Gwen and James leave slowly—to
  Maria*) You too!

- You too. (*Mr. Mac points the pistol to his
  head, pause for a moment; he drops the
  pistol and move to the liquor bar, takes
  up a bottle of brandy and takes several
  gulps. (He stumbles to the front stage)*

- My head! Oh God it's spinning, like a storm
  (*He takes another gulp from the bottle and
  staggers to his bedroom*).

BLACKOUT

ACT II

SCENE VI

The stage is completely dark; a black-light flood lamp is turned on. In addition a strobing low frequency white light comes on to give a vivid and scattered effect. Alric Mac enters from his bedroom stumbling and shouting. His wife, a ghostlike figure, flogging him with a whip.

Alric Mac

- Oh God, No! Help! Please stop!

Madge

- You nasty dog! *(Beats Alric with a whip)*

Alric Mac

- Please stop it!

Madge

- You nastiness! Your own flesh! Why did you do it! *(Continues to beat Alric after every utterance)*

Alric Mac

- It was an accident!

Madge

- Accident? Accident don't just happen, they are caused!

Alric Mac

- I don't know what caused me to do it. It must be the devil.

Madge

- Which devil, It's the devil in you own dirty spirit (*Beats*).

Alric Mac

- It happened the first and only time, it was only once.

Madge

- Yes, once and never again. (*Madge intensifies the beating. Alric shouts helplessly for mercy. He falls; Madge then goes over him, wraps the whip around his neck and chokes him*).

- *Alric lies flat and stiff. A Corpse.*

EPILOGUE

(Newsboy moves through the audience with copies of a newspaper)

Esrick

- Extra! Extra! Read all about it! On Target Daily News with the full story. Top Civil Servant found dead at his home. Local pathologists cannot state cause of death. Extra! Extra! Paper for you lady? Thank you. Yes top Civil Servant found dead no scratches no bruises, no clots. Pathologist cannot state cause of death. *(This may be repeated several times.)*

NATIONAL PLAYERS THEATRE MOVEMENT

PRESENTS FOR ITS 36TH ANNIVERSARY

WITH A BOUNCIN' WILLIAMS PRODUCTION

Ramonge Benjamin
Romaine Belgrove
Schneidman Warner
Sylvester Wattley
Reginald O'Loughlin
Jamilla Fraser
Azuree Liburd
Unoma Allen
Fiona Swanston

STORM WITHOUT BREEZE

WRITTEN / DIRECTED / PRODUCED BY
CLEMENT BOUNCIN' WILLIAMS

AT SIR CECIL JACOB'S AUDITORIUM – ECCB
ON FRIDAY 19, SATURDAY 20 AND SUNDAY 21
OCTOBER, 2012
SHOWTIME NIGHTLY 8:00 PM

ADMISSION $ 20.00 ANY SEAT

Tickets available at Dawne's Beauty Salon, Harper's Office Depot on Fort Street
and members of the National Players or Call Bouncin at 662 3899

Design Layout JPX Studio 869 667 0105

IT'S ONLY FOR A TIME

A PLAY IN ONE ACT

Written by
Clement Bouncin' Williams.

IT'S ONLY FOR A TIME

A Play in one Act

This work was first staged as a short skit in December 1968 as part of the side show to "Miss Rural Beauty Contest" held at the Sandy Point High School Auditorium. Since then it was revised and extended to a One—Act Play with staging time of approximately forty minutes in 1976.

The play is laced with comedy as it looks at many of the hypocrisies that are so common place in our societies. Even though originally written over forty years ago it is as relevant today as it was then.

This play has been staged many times throughout St. Kitts and Nevis by various groups through the years. Its home stage has been that of the National Players Theatre Movement of St. Kitts.

IT'S ONLY FOR A TIME has had many performances stage by the STROLLING PLAYERS in Trinidad and Tobago; under the direction of Freddie Kissoon and has been part of the Strolling Players repertoire for many years.

Players of the first series of production were:

John—Aubrey Heart
Mary—Marylyn Dickenson
Rupert—Henry "Stogumber" Browne
Willie—Clement "Bouncin'" Williams
Parson—Eustace "Swing" Arrindell

SCENE OPENS: Mary wife of John sits sewing one of John's pants in their one room house which contains kitchen, bedroom, etc. Mary is also singing a verse of her favourite song. John enters, holding a bottle almost full with rum in one hand, swaying from side to side. John is not really drunk he is just high.

John

- Mary love, you is the most loveliest and beautiful and charming woman in the world, and tonight we go have it like we never had it before.

  Aye . . .aye . . . *(He kisses Mary)* . . . not even like the night we did get married. *(John takes a drink)*

Mary

- Lord you aint see you getting old, why you don't behave and respect yourself. And at least you could stop drinking.

John

- Me stop drinking, well how me blood gone flow through me body? That is what keep me heart working. Anyway, tonight ah had it ding—dong.

  Ah de win two hundred and twenty five dollars ($225) in the Bingo and a put it up till tonight. Me and de boys, done blow up that in booze. Ha . . . . hay—this is the last of it now going, slowly but surely. *(John takes a big gulp of rum).*

Mary

- *(In sad and almost crying tone)* Lord John, you mean to say that it is months that you aren't working and we owe Mr. Thomas over four hundred dollars for food what we trust. The Lord was so good to bless with two hundred and twenty five dollars and you squander all of it! At least we could ah pay down something on de shop book.

John

- The same way the Lord taking care of me and lay me win two hundred and twenty five dollars, he gone take care of the shop book too.

Mary

- You go ahead, that rum gone bring you to your dooms day before long

John

- Ah don't K what your say, I know what a man love; he die for.

Mary

- You see how you making joke about the Lord and death.

John

- Is the Lord who self say that my name will be like a pillar unto thee and a comforter in the time of storm.

Mary

- The Devil and all could talk 'bout scriptures.

John

- But how you could call you sweet loving husband a devil? Why you can't call me angel or Jesus Christ? He does talk 'bout scriptures too. *(He tries to kiss Mary)*.

Mary

- *(Standing and moving away)* John as soon as you take in you rum you always have to be talking 'bout the Lord and the Bible as if you mocking. You aren't supposed to be calling the Lord's name in vain. One of these days He gone strike you down.

John

- You think the Lord is like you and them rest people. He knows exactly what to do. Is them people who do pretend that they is Christian and that they Holy; is them he does give on slap and nock them into the endless pit of fire. You see how he de do that woman from over Wash Street, who say she used to be preaching morning, noon and night.

Mary

- But John you must not judge the woman, you don't know whether she dead good or bad.

John

- But girl, it isn't no maybe 'bout that, you know where they did find she body is over to the back of the South Eastern Peninsular Road half naked. Enough people did see her and Pastor Bigstelle going driving late the afternoon before.

Mary

- But John you think is the pastor de kill her?

John

- Woman No! No doctor could ah find out what caused her death. She had no cut nor bruises on her body. Is a slap God give her and pass her on! *(John takes another drink).*

Mary

- *(Reflecting)* Oh John, You cousin Cynthie de come to you.

John

- What Cynthie looking for me for?

Mary

- Me ain't know! Because she wouldn't tell me when ah ask her.

John

- But how she looking?

Mary

- She looks like she thirteen months pregnant.

John

- Thirteen months, she must be a donkey or a elephant

Mary

- She belly look real terrible. It far out in front of her and still it twist on the

side. I sure when she look down she can't
see she . . .

John

- I know what she want. She looking money to
pay the maternity doctor.

  She don't want to stay up there in the
pen like a stray goat with she kid until
somebody come up and claim her. Ha! Ha!

Mary

- That must happen to them. They blood hot
that they have to got three—four and five
men to feel happy. In the end they get
catch and too shame to call any one of
they man name because they ain't sure.

John

- Girl de smarter ones does call de name who
working for the most money and high up in
society.

Mary

- But if they know that they moving up and
down why they don't go family planning.
They could get protectives free.

John

- They want the thing natural.

Mary

- John somehow me ain't like how Cynthie look. She look like she going bust anytime. If that was to happen, is dead she dead.

John

- *(Holding his abdomen)* Praise the Lord, I is a man and I sure one thing that pregnancy can't kill me. Ha! Ha! As I always say a man who lives by the sword will die by the sword. *(He takes another drink of rum)*

Mary

- But John you ain't bound to go on so.

John

- All I saying is that what a man love he die for. *(John takes a big gulp of rum, he strangles, coughs and vomits and falls back on to the bed—Mary runs to help him).*

Mary

- *(Tapping him)* John, John, get up, what happen to you? John, John, answer me no! . . . eh John . . . . *(Mary now realizing that John is breathless covers the body with a sheet, moves away from the bed and screams at the top of her voice)* Lord have mercy upon me, ah ain't got a soul now in this world. Lord John dead. *(Mary continues to cry for a while).*

Rupert

- *(Rushing on stage)* What it is happen to you Mary? Eh . . . . Girl? What it is?

Mary

- Lord have mercy 'tis John. Lord have mercy on me!

Rupert

- What happen, he beat you up again?

Mary

- He came home, he was not too drunk but he was sweet. Me and he start to talk so nice and he . . . he . . . take in with the bad feeling and vomiting *(sobs).*

Rupert

- And where he is now?

Mary

- Lord Rupert ah see John stretch out on the bed stiff—stiff like a cockroach. Boy he stone dead. (*Pointing at the bed; Rupert goes to and looks at the bed*).

Rupert

- You mean John—dead!—But me and he was just firing liquors together.

Mary

- Lord what ah gone do now? Ah ain't got a soul.

Rupert

- What you crazy! Look you got me. Girl, is a long time ah de love you, you know that I would do anything for you.

Mary

- You got this thing as a joke. But ah ain't got a thing to bury John with.

Rupert

- That ain't no trouble, we could get two salt fish box from Mr. Thomas and join them together and make that do for a coffin. Ah got a little money Ah could give you to pay the parson with so that he could read the burial and let the public do the rest.

Mary

- What you mean, me husband ain't worst off than anybody else.

Rupert

- Well you could go to the welfare and get a funeral grant from Social Security.

Mary

- But the Social Security grant can't even buy a decent coffin! Why he must get a pauper burial. I want a good funeral for him.

Rupert

- But girl, you ain't got the kind of money the funeral agency man does charge.

Mary

- How much so they do charge?

Rupert

- All kinds a thousands and thousands of dollars and thing. You remember that man who had the rum shop on Wash Street so he dead the other day?

Mary

- Oh yes! He funeral de look real sweet.

Rupert

- Well he had a life insurance for ten thousand dollars; and when he son done pay for the funeral, all the boy get was four hundred and fifty dollars.

Mary

- But how come?

Rupert

- The funeral man charge eight thousand five hundred dollars for the box and to keep him on the fridge for five days, four hundred for the grave spot and the grave diggers, a hundred dollars for the organist and fifty dollars for the death announcement on the radio plus four hundred for the pastor to church him and read the burial. Count up that and subtract it from ten thousand

and see if it ain't four hundred and fifty dollars he left with.

Mary

- But the priest ain't had to charge so much to read the burial.

Rupert

- You think it easy. Them fellows who say that they is priest in them high church just out to make as much money as them doctors and lawyers.

Mary

- That man used to go to church every Sunday. I sure that is a reasonable change he use to throw in the collection plate.

Rupert

- Them priests now a days ain't concern about which member throwing in de most collection. All he know is that the plate full and he get enough money to buy he liquors and Guinness to pep him up, everything all right.

Mary

- But Rupert all you doing is just talking and you ain't doing a thing 'bout John.

Rupert

- Girl I done tell you already what to do, get that parson who does preach and keep church under the lamp-post up the road to read the burial. He ain't gone charge you more than you can afford to pay. So long as he could get enough to buy a rum, everything okay.

Mary

- But Rupert, John spirit would grieve to know that he come off to a pauper burial.

Rupert

- Could afford and can't afford is two different things

Mary

- *(Sobbing)* I know . . . . But . . . . at least it would . . . ah look so nice if we could get to church him.

Rupert

- *(Almost shouting)* Girl you crazy! Church him? The only time John used to go church is when somebody dead and he go funeral, or on a Covenant Sunday when he go pray off the old year's sin. I could tell you, the thing that does really make him go to church is because the parson does share the biggest glass a wine on that day. If they church he, better they de church Lucifer.

Mary

- Anyhow, it got to work so then. Oh God, look how Ah lose me nice husband! Ah got to go all by myself now.

Rupert

- Girl you making good joke. Is long time Ah love you! I was only waiting for John to dead or go away before ah make me move. You know he was a really cantankerous man who de like he machete very much; and to tell you the truth, I was afraid of him when he was alive.

Mary

- This is serious times and you making jokes.

Rupert

- Mary darling; you think is jokes a making? Girl Ah serious till Ah can't serious no more. Mary, you know that every time Ah take a good look at you, you make me nerves stand up.

Mary

- Lord, We used to live such a nice life, we used to fight every now and then, he even cut me once or twice, but Ah never mind all these because it was fun when we making up.

  Especially when we *(Sobs)*. He was such a nice man.

Rupert

- Forget he now and talk 'bout you and me when we get married. Look see, when Ah get married to you A wouldn't touch you with a piece of straw. When Ah get me pay Ah gone bring home all me money and put it in your hand. Ah gone buy car, house, radio, television and all the nice things you want.

Mary

- But wait! You only a farm helper, getting six dollars an hour.

Rupert

- Ah think you better put handle to me work, Ah is an Agricultural-wrist that is what the Census Man de write on the voting paper.

Mary

- Well whatever Agricultural-wrist or whatever that big word is it ain't make no difference to me. Is still six dollars a hour you working for.

Rupert

- Man me boss like me, I soon gone get promotion. I might even get a chance to come the boss on the farm because they going-way soon.

Mary

- Anyhow, I done with that thing. I gone wash me pot and turn it down.

Rupert

- You mean to say that a young good looking girl like you going put yourself back on the shelf.

  Even if Ah got to do thief to make you happy. I could always get Willy or one them boys to help me out work a little bit of finger-smithery.

Willy

- *(Entering from the street)*. What you calling me name for? Just like two women always talking neager-business.

Mary

- Lord Willy, You ain't know what happen? You best friend John just dead.

Willy

- Don't make joke and we de just banging booze together down de shop.

Mary

- Boy,he dead in truth. See him cover down over there on the bed.

Willy

- *(Moving over to the bed and lifting the sheet)* Me God! He—dead—in—truth! He face done start to turn white, Ah used to hear me grandmother say have one and it make you keep alive, but nowadays it look like have a one too many and then die*(removes a flask from his pocket and take a sip)*.

Rupert

- Well boy, one garn left two. All that mean we could share the booze half-half.

Willy

- That is all you could think 'bout, rum! Anyhow, Ah gone miss him bad, because he is the only one Ah could Ah depend on for a drink. If he only had money for one, when he done drink he would even let me get a rinse of the glass to settle me nerves.

Rupert

- Well, what we gone do now?

Willy

- We got to leave everything till tomorrow, we can't go wake up the neighbours to tell them John dead. It's after hours.

Rupert

- So what we gone do?

Willy

- We could have a little wake now on the side. You got any coffee and biscuits in the house.

Mary

- Yes! I de Just boil up some coffee for John, when he come home drunk all he does want is coffee and biscuits and something else.

Willy

- Well bring them up. I have a little booze here *(pulling the flask from his pocket)* me arm! Ah find it running low *(takes a sip and puts it back in his pocket)*

Rupert

- Boy Willy, you know every time you take a sip of that you make me throat jump.

Willy

- A can't afford a drop of this. I believe in the old saying that every man sees for himself and God see for all. Aye . . . Mary, John had anything in the house?

Mary

- A believe he had a bottle in he hand when he dead.

Willy

- Well look for it. Wha' no kill fatten. It done kill one already *(Mary returns with the coffee and biscuits).*

Rupert

- It look like we gone have a ding dong time here tonight *(Mary returns with the rum and two glasses; they sit, eat and drink).*

Rupert

- *(After a moment of silence).* Well, we gone sit here silent all night?

Mary

- No man. We could talk about old times.

Willy

- Woman as usual, tell a woman don't talk is like telling a baby don't cry or one them old time cowboy bad man not to wear a gun.

Mary

- What happen to you?

Willy

- Go ahead no! She must talk 'bout the three m's that's all woman could talk 'bout, Man, Money and Marriage.

Mary

- Lord A can't forget the night that me and John get married. What sweet me so—is when the parson say 'bout to have and to hold, for better or worst and until death do us part, I hold on to him tighter for the better.

Willy

- What happen when he say for the worse

Mary

- *(Ignoring Willy)* . . . What made me nearly jump out of me frock is when John put the ring on me finger and the parson say . . ." I pronounce you man and wife."

Rupert

- John done dead and nearly gone! Let the priest say the same thing 'bout you and me. I gone treat you nice.

Willy

- Boy what happen to you? It look like you get duck soup to cook you head. I ain't in this married thing at all because I ain't agree with this thing about one woman to one man. Boy when a man married he foot tie, he ain't free to move between the chicks again.

Mary

- That is what you like eh?

Willy

- They ain't got a thing better than when you single and free. Just imagine that me eyes going be tied to watch one woman. No way! When them girls come home for Christmas and Music Festival, and they dress-up in them sexy outfits and they stepping *(he gets up to demonstrate)* Me? I must make me pass.

Mary

- All you want is to run round and taste here and taste there. You ain't seeing how much AIDS soaring in the place these days.

Willy

- AIDS is the least; just make sure that you have the necessary tools of the trade. I am never without my covers, rain or shine. *(Takes a strip with three condoms from his pocket).*

Mary

- All you men are just the same.

Willy

- I don't care what you say. I aint really got anything about marriage, but I believe if a man must get married it should be for like two years and when that time up if they like it, they go back for another two years and so on. I can't stand this thing 'bout till death do us part.

Rupert

- *(to Mary)* Don't bother with he, let we get married. I gone give you all the money you want

Willy

- You could catch she with that! Woman love money how fowl love corn. *(a parson dressed in a shabby ministerial outfit enters)*

Parson

- Good evening my friends, I have come in this time of grief and gravity. I have heard of John's death and I have come to impress my sympathy to his wife and close friends.

Rupert

- Man you couldn't hear that John dead because nobody talk the news yet.

Willy

- Man, no bother with he. He compass point out that rum here, so he reach.

Parson

- Oh yes! . . . A mean no! Arm . . . John was a good man; he was always faithful to the church. He was a good worker for the Lord even though he did come to church once a year, on that great Covenant Sunday. When he came I was sure to find at least one paper collection which was much better than some persons whom I had to talk to every Sunday and throw a lousy penny in the plate. Simple arithmetic could show that John was a more useful person than most of those people.

Rupert

- *(Pouring rum in a cup—gesturing.)* that's right parson, let's fire one on that.

Parson

- *(At first stretching his hand and then realizing.)*

  Sorry, sorry, I doesn't drinks

Rupert

- O.K then when I drink you swallow.

Parson

- For now! Arm . . . John would be missed by all in this area, because he was one of those few people who put their community before themselves. He would be missed by his lovely wife, and I am inviting you to spend some more time at the rectory now that John is dead. He would also be missed by his good buddies here and last but not least the collection would miss that glorious bank note on that bright Covenant Sunday next year.

Mary

- Lord Parson you make me feel sorry for me self and all.

Parson

- There is no need to be sorry my dear. All you need to do is put your faith and trust in me, that faith will be well with God, as I am a man of God. I'll take care of your earthly as well as your spiritual needs.

Willy

- Man you sound like you looking something.

Parson

- Never mind that . . . Now let us all sit together and sing a song suitable for the occasion. *(They sit and sing a few lines of "Abide with me" with a slow draggy pitch).* Abide with me . . . (*as they sing they are all drinking and eating the coffee and biscuits—the singing is interrupted by Mary)*

Mary

- *(Shouting)* Ah hear a noise in the corner!

Rupert

- Me arm! The Sheet Moving.

Willy

- Lazarus a rise from the dead.

  (All scatter off stage. The parson reaches the exit, but returns to collect the bottle with rum).

John

- *(Rising slowly)* Lord, this must be the coming of judgment morning.

(BLACKOUT)

The End!

THE DESIRED HONEYMOON

A ONE ACT PLAY

Written by
Clement Bouncin' Williams.

The Play

The Desired Honeymoon was written by *Clement Bouncin' Williams* after having the dream that was transferred to the character Ben. It has been becoming more and more popular for persons, who could not afford proper weddings at the time of their marriage, are now having them ten, fifteen, twenty and twenty five years later, now that the quality of life in the society has improved tremendously. Facing the issues of too much weight and the related health issues at the same time, has caused the writer, in general, to have combined these two issues in what has turned out to be the themes in the play. Along with some social commentary on issues of the day and thus offers public education on some of the major concerns about obesity.

The first draft of the play was written in one sitting of about four hours.

CAST

Ben: forty-five year old building contractor.

Agnes: forty-four year old housewife and the former manager of the Port authority cafeteria.

THE DESIRED HONEYMOON was first produced for stage in October, 2011 at the Sir Cecil Jacobs' Auditorium, Eastern Caribbean Central Bank, Bird Rock, St. Kitts by the National Players Theatre Movement.

The original cast

Fiona Swanston . . . . Agnes
Randolph Taylor . . . . Ben

Production team

Producer/Director . . . . Clement Bouncin' Williams
Stage Manager . . . . Damian Maynard
Stage Assistant . . . . Sylvester Wattley
Lighting . . . . ECCB Tech Crew

Setting: A simple verandah setting with a long couch (or bench) and a single seat off to the right and facing an open yard; it is early evening.

Agnes enters dressed in exercise wear and is doing her warm down routine from her exercise class and brisk walk back home. She speaks to her cell phone

Agnes:

- (*On cell phone with a Bluetooth ear piece, pausing here and there as if for response*) This high blood pressure and diabetes isn't going to cause me to live an unsatisfactory life style. I know I had the pressure from since I had me last child and I am continuing to take me medications every morning, the first thing as I get up. The doctors over the last five years or so have been telling me that I need to lose some weight and that will help to keep the blood pressure under control. Hypertension runs deep on both sides of me family so it is no surprise that I am suffering from it. Losing weight is one of the most difficult things. My last physical examination said that my sugar is now border line and that I am a prime candidate for type 2 diabetes and that I could beat it off by sticking to a good exercise regime and diet. I am afraid of diabetes too bad. The blindness and losing one or both feet and legs just horrify me. My physician said that I should talk to a specialist dietician, so I went to see this good lady. A very pleasant meeting; she asked me to try and recall all that I had eaten over the last three days. I called out and she listed. Lord, when I look at the list, I was so ashamed of myself. I would not even recite them again, not even if I was on stage acting. She evaluated the calorific content of my ingestions, that is the terms she used; a never hear more thousands of calories. That is really excessive she said. I frighten so till. She started to measure me as if

145

she was a seamstress. Buss one hundred and ten. I shout out no, you measurement isn't right I am size 44; yes that is in inches but I use the international metric system, which is 110 centimetres, waist 85 and hips 130. I don't like them metric measurement; people who don't know, would think it was an elephant they was measuring. I like the weight in metric because I was just 101. That is in kilograms. Finally she gave me a book to record everything that I ate for a week, as well as the exercise and activities I did. That took me aback; I had to ask her if she meant the very personal activities too, she said no. She said don't worry about personal activities as such, that could only help to better your health and wellness. The dietician gave me a guide book about the importance of a balanced diet, to have a good balance between starches, proteins, and especially, vegetables and fruits which are the main sources of vitamins and minerals which are essential for the healthy maintenance of the body by strengthening the immune system. She also said that the body needs plenty of water to flush the systems, both alimentary and urinary tracts.(*Removes the Bluetooth device from her ear and hides it from Ben*)

Ben:

- (*Coming from within the house*) who you talking to? I hear you voice out here and did not hear anybody answering back.

Agnes:

- It is me, just letting off some steam.

Ben:

- (*Showing some concern*)Well at least I know that you aren't crazy because you never answer back to the questions you were asking. What happen to me food, that small ball of cornmeal? That thing was just as big as the size of my fist.

Agnes:

- That is the perfect quantity for you to eat boy. The dietician say that our starch quantities must be as big as our fist and should be able to hold in the palm of your left hand, (*She demonstrates all the suggestions*) the proteins should be able to sit across the four finger and as much fruits and vegetables that could fit in the space between your thumb and index finger. Imagine that you left hand is you plate; and if it can't hold don't eat it.

Ben:

- The snapper was good, it extended outside the plate.(*He demonstrates*)

Agnes:

- That is okay, we should eat as much fish as we could, and don't throw away the skin, that have in some of the essential oils and fats like omega 3, 6 and 9 that are required by the body to carry out the metabolic functions properly.

Ben:

- I still hungry; you haven't got any more food inside.

Agnes:

- No, that is the advice of the dietician, that I should cook only the food that we need to eat; if there is extras we will eat that as well. I find that is good advice, especially these days when VAT makes the price of food so expensive. Here drink some water to full up your stomach that would ease the hunger till later.

Ben:

- Girl, I am not thirsty I hungry. Is food I want to eat!

Agnes:

- Well Ben you gone have to adjust to the new dietary style and portions we gone be following.

Ben

- *(Ben shrugs his shoulders in disgust and sucks on his teeth)* S-t-u-p-s!

Agnes

- But where you pick up?

Ben:

- I send Mack over Conaree to do something for the Charles'. He dropped me off here and gone to do what they want him to do. When he finish he will call me and I will tell him where to find me.

Agnes:

- That is why I never realize that you were inside. *(In an aggressive and amorous mood, crouches up to Ben and rubs his head)* If I knew that you were in there in the bed I would have come in to trouble you.

Ben:

- (*A bit pensive*) Girl this afternoon I had a nap and had a dream that seem so funny to me.

Agnes:

- What dream that could be that have you so bassidy?

Ben:

- I dream that you plan for us to get married again on we twenty-fifth anniversary.

Agnes:

- Good idea, that gone be next April. April 5,198? (*Adjust the year to correspond to twenty five years from present.*)—was the date we got married; that will make exactly twenty five years since I commit myself to you in the presence of the judge and man. I have kept the estate of God holy, I love you, I cherish you, I cook you food every day, wash your clothes. Every week by Sunday afternoon I have you five uniform shirts pressed and on hangers for you to go to work in for the week. I have kept myself unto thyself and to you only; I isn't sure if I could say the same thing 'bout you.

Ben:

- *(Shocked at the response)* What I did to deserve this kind of a tongue lashing at this hour of the day? I simply tell you about a dream I had just a while ago.

Agnes:

- Yes, and it is an idea I had been thinking about and I was wondering how I would approach you with it. It has to be the right thing to do; the Lord himself put that vision in your mind and directs you to come and tell me.

Ben:

- But this isn't the first time a tell you about a dream, so what so special about this one?

Agnes:

- When we got married how old I was?

Ben:

- Nineteen.

Agnes:

- How old you were?

Ben:

- Twenty.

Agnes:

- You remember what happened?

Ben:

- What this about now? We were friends since in school, since we were little!

Agnes:

- In grade six, in Mrs Thomas class, that is all when it began. You remember how I used to help you with you spellings when Mrs Thomas gave us the wordlist to learn. I used to want to bawl when she used to beat you for the amount of faults you had in you dictation.

Ben:

- But I used to show you how to do the maths them too.

Agnes:

- Yes, and we were "friendsing" all the way through high school, helping each other.

Ben:

- It ain't much help I could have given you, only in maths. The other subjects that I did and was good in were Woodwork, Technical Drawing and Electricity and you never did them.

Agnes:

- Ben, you provided me with security, I never had any trouble from anybody in school. You remember how Rags and they use to bully them girls and take away their money and other things. I was never bothered because my protector was always on hand. We left school together, and went Technical College together; you did Construction Technology and what I did?

Ben:

- Home Economics and Tourism Management.

Agnes:

- We work hard and we get our City and Guilds Certificates.

Ben:

- I could remember the days when you made me study when I wanted to go liming with Rags and them boys. You put some heavy sanctions on me you know. I couldn't even touch you never mind to get a kiss from you those days if we did not study together for two to three hours daily. Many a days I was ready to give up college and hit the streets.

Agnes:

- To follow Rags and the other purple (rude boys) them, Where Rags is today?

Ben:

- In Her Majesty's Prison serving fifteen years for armed robbery and attempted murder along with Coop and Manuel.

Agnes:

- And if you had your own way, I sure you would have been the fourth member in that gang. When we leave college I got the job at the front desk of the hotel. Then a little while later you went to work with Jenkins' Construction.

Ben:

- I learnt a lot from that man, and I will have eternal respect and gratitude for him; may his soul rest in peace (*makes the sign of the cross*).

Agnes:

- You realise that we were out of School and working for just three months before I got pregnant.

Ben:

- Don't blame me, blame the spirit of Christmas and Carnival and the music of Elli Matt and the GI's Brass; after that dance at the Factory Social Centre, you could not wait. I told you not to drink that Guinness.

Agnes:

- Ben, I have no regrets, I got pregnant and you stood with me every step of the way; you were the one who went and told my mother what was happening. I thought she would have made a fuss, but she took it in stride. She commented that she expected this sooner or later. You know momma always liked you!

Ben:

- She was a nice lady; she always welcomed me, since from the days of primary school.

Agnes:

- We decided to get married, no bank account, nothing but the love we had for each other. We could not even afford a new dress for me; I got married in the uniform of the Fort Thomas Hotel front desk. The Registrar of the High Courts administered the oaths of matrimony in the presence of the judge; we signed the register, with your father and my mother as witness. We left the Court House and went to the square where we had a brief conversation and getting their blessings and congratulations; all four of us headed off in the four different directions, you went east to a construction site on Pond's Pasture, Momma went west through central street to do some shopping, your father went north to get back to the sugar factory where he worked and I headed south to the Bay Road to head back to the Fort Thomas Hotel. I could remember strutting with pride with a little stiffness on my left hand, smiling all the way back to my place of work, repeating my new name to myself, Agnes Evelyn Murray. Everyone whom I encountered that day wanted to know what had become over me; I motioned with a gentle wave of my left hand, and the shining tinkle of ten carat gold was sufficient to reveal the story. I could not wait to sign my first dispatch order; I had been practicing my new signature since I can't remember when.

Ben:

- Girl I was frightened you know, when I thought of the responsibility of wife and child. You realized that we got married and went back home, you to your mother's and me back to my father's house.

Agnes:

- We made it Ben, together. When Justin was born on the 16th of September that year, the same date as the Right Excellence Sir Robert Llewellyn Bradshaw our first National Hero, I was the happiest human being on planet Earth. It was a day that I had dreamt of since back in Mrs Thomas grade six.

Ben:

- That's typical of all women, their desire of becoming a bride and a mother.

Agnes:

- You realize that it was not until some months after Justin's birth that we actually rented a two room house and made our first home; where we lived together and slept in the same bed. Now today, we have we own place, thanks to the government. We got a low income house, and you with your trade, we were able to do addition after addition until today; look at what we got, a four bedroom house with an adjoining studio apartment on rent, bringing in some revenue. Ben we have a lot to be thankful for.

Ben:

- What you want us to married over for? We living good all these years, you don't hear old people say that if it is not broken don't try to fix it. Agnes, it' working.

Agnes:

- We are not going to change a thing; all I desire is a wedding ceremony in a church, a honeymoon and a classy fete. I am not asking for anything that you cannot afford!

Ben:

- Ok, Ok, you work out the maths and let me know.

Agnes:

- That is the point I making; look how long this partnership and cooperation going on for. We never had much but we always shared what little we got with each other. Ben we gone get married again, this time the right way!

Ben:

- I ain't so sure that I want to go through all that kind of problems. But anyhow it's for you!

Agnes:

- It isn't going to be no problem for you; I will make all the arrangements necessary for our second matrimony in the sight and presence of our Lord. Ben, it is going to be in the Church and not in the Court House, not in the dens of liars, thieves and murderers; like the first one was. I gone get your cousin, the Cannon Reverend Father Isaiah Phillip, to do the ceremony for us and for him to give us the blessings for at least another twenty five years more.

Ben:

- Man you sound like you gone make something like the Royal Wedding of the Duke and Dutchess of Cambridge, Prince William and Lady Catherine.

Agnes:

- (*Emphatically*) I am not going to invite the Queen, but her representative on hand, his Excellency the Governor General will be invited. Wait, a wonder if he will give me away? My father and mother done dead, so he is the fittest and most proper person to give me away, he is all of us father. You remember he delivered me with our first son.

Ben:

- Girl you think he gone remember you for that, he done deliver thousands of babies already, what was so special about you, why you think he gone remember you?

Agnes:

- He must remember me, you know is years I work at the front desk and then at the bar at the old Fort Thomas Hotel. Those were the days when he was still on the prowl. I always treated him with the greatest dignity and courtesy whenever it was he and his friends who came to the hotel; whether he was in company or by himself. Many nights he sat at the bar, sipping a drinking waiting for a call from the hospital's maternity ward. He always had something to say.

Ben:

- But Agnes, you sound like this gone cost a lot of money

Agnes:

- I ain't work out the budget yet for the wedding. I want us to have a breakfast reception at the Marriott and not one soul more than a hundred persons, only close family and good friends. Then we gone fly out on the American Airlines jet from RLB to Miami to join a cruise on one of the Carnival Fun ships. A seven day cruise of the Western Caribbean and Central America for our desired honeymoon.

Ben:

- A hundred persons, at the Marriott, way we gone get that kind of money from. Seven days cruise for honeymoon, hem—seven days, that gone make a whole week.

Agnes:

- I ready for that. Don't worry, I done set aside some of me Port Authority redundancy money in Government Treasury Bonds, the interest growing all the time at eight percent (8%) and the maturity date is March 30. Just in time for the occasion.

Ben:

- But you never tell me about those Treasury Bonds, how much in them?

Agnes:

- You don't worry about that!

Ben:

- But I should know, I am your husband,
  suppose something happen to you? The
  Government would just take you money; all
  will be gone for nothing.

Agnes:

- No Ben, I have the money stated as I T F,
  in trust for you, Benjamin O. Murray. The
  money would come automatically to you.

Ben:

- You sure?

Agnes:

- As sure as there is a god.

Ben:

- Agnes, give me seven dollars.

Agnes:

- What you want seven dollars for?

Ben:

- I have to answer that question? You loving husband ask you for a measly, one, two, three, four, five, six, seven dollars and I have to give an account for it.

Agnes:

- *(Reaches in her pocket and takes out a small purse, opens it and takes out a five dollar note and two one dollar coins and hands it to Ben).*

Ben:

- Thank you very much, you gone save me life.

Agnes:

- What you mean by that?

Ben:

- After all that talk, and the little piece of food you left for me, I hungry like hell. I going down the road to buy a seven dollar Chinese food.

Agnes:

- Ben no! That food full up of bad cholesterol. *(In a sarcastic tone)* go ahead, go ahead and see if I don't bury you early.

Ben:

- You will cry and bawl for a while but when you get the life insurance money from me National Insurance policy you will be smiling all the way to the bank. *(Ben exits the stage).*

(Blackout)

EPILOGUE

Agnes

- *(Dressed in shorts and honeymoon T shirt with straw hat, sun shades, shoulder bag and camera, runs on stage)* Ben, Ben come, come boy take me picture, I want evidence.

Ben

- *(Dressed in shorts and honeymoon T shirt with straw hat, sun shades up on fore head and camera with telephoto SLR lens, enters shortly behind Agnes as she poses with posters with scenery and names of four ports of call)* Pose girl, smile, and say cheese. *(After some moments they hug each other front centre stage.)*

Agnes

- Ben, when we going back?

Ben

- Maybe in the next twenty five years!

Agnes

- Ben no! No! No!*(they both exit)*

BLACKOUT

MY EARLY LIFE ON St. KITTS AND NEVIS

Clement "Bouncin" Williams

AN AUTOBIOGRAPHY OF THE FIRST 22 YEARS